# POETIC
# HEAVEN
# OR HELL

# POETIC HEAVEN OR HELL

Donald Seick

**ARPress**
ILLUMINATING IDEAS,
EMPOWERING VOICES

**ARPress**
45 Dan Road Suite 5
Canton MA 02021

Hotline:        1(888) 821-0229
Fax:            1(508) 545-7580

Ordering Information:

Quantity sales. Special discounts are available on quantity purchases by corporations, associations, and others. For details, contact the publisher at the address above.

Printed in the United States of America.

ISBN-13:        Paperback        979-8-89330-126-7
                eBook            979-8-89330-127-4

Library of Congress Control Number: 2024901289

# Table of Contents

"Elohime" & "El" means "God"
"Gehenna" means "Hell"
"Abba" means "Father"

# A Freighting Feeling

**By Don Seick**

Abba, you show me things day after day
What a beautiful feeling I must say
Understanding, I must change my ways
I plead; I need!
All these changes to be ratified through you
Your blessings on all that I do
At fifty-one, I know my life is more or less at least half done
I've been pretty well blessed, or am I a weed?
Being blessed with the rest
At times, I feel you hear my prayers
Then in my sin, I wonder why would or should you care
I wasted so much time
Lost in doing what I thought was fun
Lost in doing, what was helpful to absolutely no one!
It's a frightening feeling to say in the least
To know, I've done nothing at all, but to feed the beast!
In someday I know, I will stand before El
In and with my life, where I've done nothing well
Not one decent thing am I able to bring
To the judgment that puts me in Heaven or Hell!
All my deeds are filled with shame
And the truth is, my heart is completely to blame
If it weren't for you through your Son
My whole life!
Would have been lived to Ha-Satan
Someday, in someway
I hope to see your Heavenly light, by doing in my life what's right
To know what it's like to live for you, in all, that I think say and do.

# A Great Man, Once Said
# "Let Freedom Ring"

**By Don Seick**

Freedom is such a fragile thing
If you don't take care of her, she'll flee like wings
Freedom can be a lovely fling, freedom can be a deadly thing
Many Men and Women have cried for her
Many Men Women have died for her
If you listen, you can hear her sing her glorious song
Freedom, is what makes our Nation strong
As through the generations, she's passed on and on
The blood, the sweat, the pain and tears
That's how freedom remains strong, through the years
At the birth of this Nation, I saw the price, you'd pay
Day after day the price was high, but I knew you could and would
With your lives you'd pay, and as a Nation, you were on your way
Wherever freedom called, she was answered by American resolve
Freedom will ring, as she sings her song
Proud of you all, because to me, you all belong
As we know, most Politicians, not all, to be sure, are looking for reasons
To treat my People, like thave committed treason
Beware! In that day, when tranny reigns! Where our liberties are eaten,
for our God! Given rights, we'll be beaten
The lies, of some so-called leaders, are told with pride
So many laws they pass, as they say with pride in the lie
"It's for your protection! We take these freedoms away
An American friend, a Patriot once said
"To give up your liberty, for safety's sake, is to give up your freedom"
An American disgrace!
My people, don't sit there as the beast moves in, a proud Nation
Can become weaklings and hens!
Immorality and violence, all through the land
Mass murders and killings, they have to stop!

Our American pride, for some, have been lost
Wake up my people, while we still can
We have to Trump, our rights, day by day, it will only get worse
If we don't stand and say, Enough! You have to Vote!
to stop taking our freedoms away, as a nation, we'll find our way
as a Nation, together, we'll fight our enemies, like we always have
Men and Women, Brothers and Sisters, Friends, and Neighbors
We'll fight shoulder to shoulder, bolder and bolder
We have, we can, and we'll do it again and again, by God! Amen
For liberty and freedom whatever it takes, waking this giant
Is our enemy's mistake, even if that enemy, is from within!
We don't need the Government, to run our lives
We need a good working Government, for our country to survive
If you love your freedom, there's still enough time,
to save our Nation, make up your mind!
God is our only hope, to keep this Nation from burning in smoke
It's no joke, it'll take back bone, to fight our leaders at home
To open the doors, they have already shut, the Vote! Is our weapon
Vote with your gut before it's too late, before our children,
are raised to mistake, raised to believe, our freedoms are wrong
It won't be long, and they'll all be gone
I was there when our colors were chosen, the Red, White, and Blue
Even in this, you've aloud, our leaders,
to deface me, disgrace me, to trim me in gold!
The sting of a counterfeit thing!
The Stars; they represent so many, "One for all and all for one"
Were all Mothers and Fathers, Daughters and Sons
Brothers and Sisters! Friends, and Neighbors, together were strong!
The Crimson red; "The life of the creature, is in the blood"
The love of the creature, is the blood
From the very beginning, I have seen it, every Man and Woman
Who sacrificed it all, so many warriors, in so many ways

So many warriors, in so many gravies
Land, sea, and air, they all serve, because they care
Law Enforcement and Fire fighters all our first responders
Rescuers and Searchers, Doctors and Nurses, EMS too,
Every drop of their blood, their sacrifices and all they do,
they do, for me and you
While living and working, there are those who die
They are all precious to me, and to those who cry
Families who bare a terrible loss, for you and I
To sacrifice for each other, is the American way
I thank you all each and every day, and yes
I watch as some of you deface me, disgrace, and burn me too
The crimson red, that of the dead
The crippled and broken hearted and so many more
Their sacrifices, allow you to do what you do, and so much more
And Yes, I feel your hurting too
The White; Purity, I see it in so many
The purity of love and respect, shown in so many ways
Floods, Hurricanes, Earthquakes, and more, and yes, even in wars!
So many people coming together, all the more
All races and creeds, people in need, all the religions, people believe
To help each other anyway we can
From one end to the other, of this great and marvelous land
The Blue; Is for all you do
Your families, your friends the day to day living at work and at play
Remembering to help those who legally emigrated, along the way
The freedom to come and go, to do as you like
The freedom, we Americans share in life
I've seen my people, as a third world country
Turn sticks and bricks, into a beautiful and great Nation
You fought hard! To cast the horrors of slavery aside

Black and white, many died, Civil War! Pain of the suffering still
survives
So many black lives pay a price, so many black lives still in strife
I saw the towers come down, the tears did too
Don't let the tears turn to the fear, that can bring a nation down
Again, my Children times a wasting, God! We must have back
As one Nation under God, or face that one Gods, punishing wrath
I see our Nation, as I'm flying high, stand beside me in American pride
Don't loose sight of me nor yourself
God and Country, are our home, God and Country, of our own
Freedom! She's a wonderful thing to sweet to lose
Thank you all of every Race, every Creed, and of every belief and color
For listening to me, about my need, to keep this Country strong
God! Bless America! And Bless you too!
Alongside God, old Glory, your Flag!
Watching over YOU!

# A Painful Gift

**By Don Seick**

Who of you, would or could do, as I have done?
Who could take a tender young plant, by the root;
And set it in the burning Sun?
No form of splendor, nor appearance to know
That this stricken, smitten, afflicted plant, of sickness and in pain
Is for you people, to pick from it, for healing your pain and shame!
Pierced! For your transgressions, crushed for your crookedness
By his stripes, you were healed, by his stripes, he was revealed
Like sheep who went astray
Each one of you, turned to do your own way
Your crookedness's, I laid on him, for your salvation to begin
Oppressed and afflicted, never opening his mouth!
With a terrible bloody beating, for your Brother;
There was never a doubt, for mercy, he never cried out!
My Son, was stricken by the strong
Appointed to the grave, of the rich and Wrong
Guilty of no violence or deceit, no lying, cheating, nor sin of his own!
I, his Abba, was pleased to crush! Him; for you to enter my Home
To watch him give up his life, as he made himself a sacrifice
To make your sins, white as snow
I gave him the sickness of sin, so sin could let you go
I saw a seed, and I will prolong his days
As I esteem the righteousness of his ways
As the pleasure of my prosper, is in his hands
The pleasure of my prosper, is the salvation of Man
You will now see the result of his suffering, he accomplished for me
By his stripes, my righteous servant
Made so many others righteous too
Counted with the transgressors, he bore their many sins
Unto Death! He poured out his being, to show his love
To give life meaning from above

I gave him the World and the Stares
Because the World gave him it's painful scars
King of Kings! Master of Masters!
Heaven sent the Son of Man, to make intercession, to take a stand
To enact a Heavenly plan
Through my precious son, I am happy For the Salvation
The Painful Gift! He gave to Man

# Abbas Children

### By Don Seick

I see all the starving children all over all the world
Lifeless little eyes, and their cold dead stares
No tears of pain, to water their eyes
No fear of death, they don't ever wonder why
From the pain of hunger, they don't even cry
To them it seems right
After the long hot day comes the cold lonely night
Fat little bellies, not from eating food
It's a sign this Childs life is almost through!
A child in hunger dying this way
So coldly evil and cruel
Surly in some day, in some way, the whole world will pay
Abbas gonna remember what we could and didn't do
Abba could be upset with both me and you
Now is the time to make a difference
To pray our prayers with love and indifference
Through our prayers, Abbas goanna know
If we made a show, and just how much, or if we even care
Look around this world, there's no time to spare
Judgment day is coming, will you be scared?
For these little children, Abba does care
These little babies and their cold dead stares
They don't look for help, they don't know what help is
The joy of life, they have no idea
They'd love to play, if they knew what that was
They only know a world without love
Hugs would feel good, if they didn't hurt so much
Their bodies so soft and hearts so tough!
These things must come to pass
Is what the Scriptures say, the birth pangs, of a new and better way
There are those who really do care

Their lives with these children, their willing to share
The proof of love, is the do in doing
May Abba bless these children in their pain
In our hearts and prayers may they all remain.

# You Did Not Spare

**By Don Seick**

Abba, I'm looking to tell you, wanting to say
How I want in my life, day by day, to live your way
I've seen what you do, and read about the past
I'm looking for changes, in my life that will last
Sometimes excited!
I see you; I fell you all around, sometimes sadly
I can't see or fell you; I've fallen down
Wishing life was easy, but it's not for me
I know it's my fault, I'd have to be blind not to see
I hate to fall, to miss your call
To leave my needs to burn with the weeds
For the Power of the Spirit from on High, I cry!
Not getting any younger day by day
I'm afraid I won't change, as my life slips away
I'm blessed I am, a physical Man in a physical land
Spiritually speaking, I'm at war!
A battle to the death, my heart so torn
Bleeding with need for your spiritual rest
No peace, no shalom
Like I'm fighting through life, All on my own
Here and there, I see some light, enough to ease some of the fright
On my knees! I plead my needs!
All the while, trying to say, in so many ways
Thank you, Abba, for creating me, thank you for your care of me
Thank you for your Son, who's life for the World, you did not spare
I could say, thank you for this and that all day long
Still, it wouldn't make up for all my wrongs
I can't find the words when I try to pray,
Don't know, are words enough, just to say
I love you, I do
May all your Blessings, please be on me in every way
The way your Blessings, have been on your Son
Each and every Day

# Are Your Thoughts Your Own?

**By Don Seick**

I can enter your dreams while you sleep in your bed
Twisting the truth, you think the dream said!
I'm running your brain-dead head!
You're so stupidly smart, so close to spiritual death
Can you smell, my Satanic breath?
As the Son of perdition, I've been judged
In a short matter of time, you'll be too
But until that time
If your mindless mind, is all mine, you lose!
I'll rob, rape, and murder you too
You'll do whatever I want you to do!
I'll make you think your thoughts are your own, as long as I can
I won't leave you alone, I'll see to it Gehenna's your home
And there is nothing you can do!
Unless, you know Els word, do you know Els word?
Did you know through obedient prayer and fasting?
I can, I have, I will lose!
You don't know nothing but the lust of money, drugs, and booze
It's bedtime now, come dream in the light of my night
The Angle of light, who lives by the loss of your soul
As to Hell, I want to watch you go!
If I'm in your head, your almost dead, and you're too stupid to know
I can't wait to steal, to take
You're self damned worthless soul
See you in Hell, your loss is my gain, come play
My evil maddening, Satanic game!

# Cold Dead Asleep!

**By Don Seick**

I'M dead in a place, you forsake
All because of your said mistake
Oh! Don't worry, I'm not alone
In this abyss of not a home
There are many others, torn out of the womb
By their Mothers
Throne away day after day
One more Child wasted away
Boys and Girls
So many denied life in your World
With all my heart, I hope your happy
And someone loves you
I would have been happy, loving you too
But; As it is!
You were my voice, and by your choice
Here I lay
Not at home or at peace
But; Cold Dead Asleep!
A Daughter or Son of absolutely
NO ONE!

# Day After Day

**By Don Seick**

I find myself nervous, not knowing what to say
Life has me feeling like running away
My job, the bills, I've just been divorced
Lonely and scared, I'm off my course
What should I do? what can I say?
I know, I just can't keep living this way
Can't eat or sleep, I'm tired all the time
If something don't change, I'll lose my mind!
My Daughter she calls, just to say Hi
But it takes more than that to know your alive
She asks, "Dad, how you doing, are you feeling alright?
I answer her back with a mouth full of lies
As the heart cries, through the eyes
I hang up the phone, still alone
Nerves are shaking down to my bones
I've got to change something, in living my life
I've got to find something, for me that's right
You know, I've heard it said
Prayers, fasting and tears can clear the head
Abba, my Father, I'm turning to you!
Through the name of your Son, please! What do I do?
In prayer I'll find peace, is what they say
Your peace I need, day after day
I need to calm down and take things slow
To wait for your answer, in my heart to show
What I need is the truth, that only you know
Thank you, dear Abba,
For loving me so

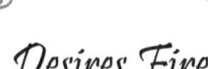

# Desires Fire

**By Don Seick**

The evil in me, I sought it, I searched it out, without a doubt
I put it in my heart, the evil inclination, was with me from the start
As a baby, a child, a young boy, I was wild
As a young man, I was mad with evil desire!
An eruption of destruction! A volcano, burning in me!
I wanted, I needed, to destroy the noise from Heaven above
To destroy any and everything! To do with Els love
When I opened my eyes, to my surprise
It was like the eyes of Messiah! We're looking through me
His burning love, ate my hate, all my mistakes were gone
Our sins, we give to him, for salvation to begin
And all he wants from us? Is to show we care
By giving our love to one another, and to his Abba above?
King of Kings, The creator of creation
The maker of the master plan
Enacted, through The Son of Man

# Free to Be Born

**By Don Seick**

Just another baby, who wasn't born
From my mother's womb, I was torn
The pain and suffering, that I felt
If you really knew, your heart would melt
You see, I believe I had the right, Abba gave me!
Like you, free to be born!
My heart and spirit, already formed
I had no choice, you were my voice
The whole World waiting for me, can't you see?
What you did to me, should never be!
It's not! Your right to kill!
To take the life, through you, Abba gave me!
MURDER! In cold blooded, cold love
You murdered me!
To be free of responsibility
I hope you're as happy as can be
I hope you can live with what you did to me!
Someday with my Abba,
you will see me again, and learn my name
I'll tell him, how I forgive you, in spite of you
Because of my love for him
My love for you? I give to him, who took my pain
I will pray for his forgiveness,
For you and your Shame!

# Heart of Gold

**By Don Seick**

My Mama, has a heart of gold, Even though she's not very old
My Mama, does a lot of good, without even being told
My Mama, she loves her Mom and Dad too
Her siblings, she'd hate to lose
For them, anything they asked, she would do
She's so happy, going in and out the door
How could any Baby want or ask for anything more?
To be born to my Mother, is all I wanted! That's what kept me warm
Knowing that someday, into Mamas arms, I'd be born
Oh, the pain! The Heartache! How I Hate!
That from my Mother's womb, I was torn!
Aborted me? I won't be born? How can that be!
My Mother loves everything, everything but me?
My Mama has a heart of gold
But to me, she was heartlessly cold!
Couldn't you feel me Mama? Couldn't you hear my cry?
I was fighting for my life!
And all you wanted was for me to die?
Thank you, Mom!
For your old, cold heart of gold

# Angles Came

**By Don Seick**

If the angles of Abba, were to come to your house
Would they eat your food, and drink your wine?
Or would they leave, and you never knew, their visit
Was but a measure of love, in time?
"For I looked into the Earth, and I did not find
Anyone worthy, not one was mine"
What are we doing with our belief?
Is it a matter of what we want, or what we think?
If so, I know, our hearts are filled, with Gehenna's stink!
Shakespeare said, "Gehenna is empty, all the Devils are here"
What in our lives do we hold dear? What in our lives do we truly fear?
Murder and fame, killing and pain
Will man ever see the evil in Satan's, Satanic game?
Temptation to evil is all he can do, the fulfillment of evil
Is in the heart, of me and you
Looking at the world, I'm so sad, surely you are too, but this is nothing
Compared to what evil, really wants from me and you to do!
Evil wants to kill and take, rape and hate, to destroy Els plan
We've got to understand, Satan hates any and everything
To do with Abbas love for man. Brothers and Sisters
Through the love of flesh, the flesh will burn and die
Materialistic gain above all, is the ruin for you and I
The flame, will bring Gehenna's pain, and in our hearts
Will burn the fires flame
Through the fall, we'll lose it all
To where the flesh is dead, and the spirit will die!
It will then be too late to pray and cry
The spirit of El, has been given to man, as part of his overall plan
To help us to help ourselves, and someone else along the way
To help us from burning in Gehenna, in the justice of the judgment
day!

It was said, "There is no greater honor, than to die, for one's friends"
Then what is the honor of him, by who he was sent?
On the day the angles come our way
I hope were ready, I hope were strong
I hope were singing with the angles
To El, all day long

# In it We all Share

**By Don Seick**

Abba, I thank you for blessing me, with the knowledge of your Son
Sent to save us, did he
The blood from his viens, the beatings and pain
His loving you and me, all of us the same
He walked in this world, dressed in our flesh
To carry our sins, to give us a rest
To the steak of execution, was his resolution
His cries, his prayers, our sins he bared
He gave up his spirit, because he cared
His blood washed the earth, in it we all share
His death and resurrection, a life of perfection
Our Messiah, love him if you will, you can't pay him back
The kingdom that was, is the kingdom that is
The kingdom to come, the kingdom he'll share, with his chosen ones
Those are the children, who show him they care
By saying and doing, the things that he shared
Love, for loves sake
Is what makes it worthwhile, that's what bring our Messiah
His beautiful smile

# Inequity's Un- Holy King

**By Don Seick**

A hot-tempered man, is what I am
A spirit, given to anger, A spirit of evil and danger!
Don't walk with me or learn my ways
Least you fall, and pay in that day, in a way you'll always regret
I give you my pledge, you'll burn on my bed
A knife, I'll put to your throat
For I am a beast, of great appetite, full of deceptive foods
Consider me, and you will learn, I will watch you burn!
Father, of the false prophet, The Beast! Of the earth
Satan the Devil
The Son of perdition, with a mission of sedition, for everyone
I'll fill you heart, with the drink of envy, the lust of another man's gold
You'll live your life, and feel it's right, fearing to grow old
Filled with pride, till the day you die, from the dark side, if all goes well
Welcome to Hell! The pit of fury's fire!
Filled, with all your burning desires
And the things you did or didn't earn
No one to hear you shout, nor care if you cry
No doubt, this is where the spirit dies!
Then you'll remember what I said, I warned you! I told you what I'd
do, I'd watch you burn, too late to learn?
His ways or mine? It's your last chance to choose
Do you even know his ways? Have you ever read his book?
Or are you content with me, to be mine?
If so, don't bother to look at his book, for in my sin, I've got you
hooked
And your flesh and bones, will burn fine!
To those, who live for me, careless men, your Father in sin
Ha-Satan, the Devil in your life
The Dragon of your dreams, the terror of your fright
The darkest Evil in the night

I'll give you, your heart's desire, but then, your soul belongs to me!
I'll watch you burn, while you scream and squirm!
You should, have simply learned, the one true thing that I said
You should have read his book
Stuck on my hook? my eternal worm
Inequity's Un-Holy King!

# Jealousy

By Don Seick

Jealousy is a monster of life
It creates fear, competitiveness, a critical spirit and strife
Jealousy is a divided mind of anger and pain
The shame of jealousy, is always the same
Jealousy easily takes offence
To defend insecurity, disorder, and confusion
Jealousy leads to sin, loss of focus and illusion
Enmity, between family and friends
Jealousy causes loss of energy and will
Physical illness and hate that can Kill!
Jealousy will steal and rob you blind
Each and every
Hurtful, Hateful, Satanic time

# Life

**By Don Seick**

Life is funny, and can be cruel
Life, can be a mixed-up blessing from you
Life is sad, the hard times a challenge
But in most ways Abba, life's a joy, life's a breeze
Life flows quickly, Like A Breeze through the trees
Beautiful to watch, so violent to the leaves
Life is fragile, so easy to flee
Thank you, Abba, for the life in me
And all the life, I've been blessed to see
Bless our Messiah, and his spirit too
But most of all Abba, is there a blessing I can say
That blesses you too?
For all the wonderful things in life
You from Heaven do

# Life, Through Pain Suffering And Death

**By Don Seick**

Messiah my savior, what can I say
I try to find ways day after day
To see in my mind, the lives you saved
To feel in my heart, the price you paid
To feel your pain, and know your sorrow
Always wondering about tomorrow
Trying to understand, why you gave your life
For the likes of sinful Man
You Offer us your Sabbath Rest
You healed the sick and raised the dead
While you, the Son of Man
Had nowhere, to lay your head
You cast out Demons, by love and Prayer
You taught the good news everywhere
We scrounged you, beat you, we spit in your face
Like wild animals locked in a cage
Our hearts filled with evils rage
We called you a liar
For whose Son, you say you are
We beat you with whip's, ripping your flesh
So much torture without a rest
Still, your forgiving, in unselfishness
We put a crown of thorns upon your head
Just to see your face run blood red
On the road to death, with all our hearts
We hated you and your word from the start
That was the reason for the beating and pain
In our world you couldn't remain
Out of unselfish love
You carried our steak, to your execution
We didn't know, we didn't care, it was for our salvation

We loved watching you in pain, and humiliation
You fell to the ground time after time
Black and blue, so bloody too!
We laughed, being Els Son, is this the best you can do?
As you looked us all in the eyes, searching for compassion
It really should have been no surprise
All you got was hate, in the crowd's reaction
Seeing you suffer, and hearing your pain
This is why the crowd remained!
As the Centurions continued exposing your bones
The crowd continued a party of their own
We hung you on a Tree, for the whole World to see
Pounding nine-inch nails, into your hands and feet
We watched you squirm in pain and defeat
Little did we know, how precious your Blood
As we watched it flow
Still laughing, we sighed, at the Man of lies
If you're Els Son, the Messiah you say!
Come off that Tree, your own life won't you save?
With more laughter and jokes, we rolled dice for you cloak
When you asked us for water, something to drink?
We gave you vinegar, rotten with stink
Out of your body flowed water and blood
And still you said,
"Abba forgive them" in mercy and Love
What could you have possibly, been thinking of?
Eternal life! With all! Your willing to share?
Through giving your life, though not many cared
"Abba, into your hands, I commit my spirit, it is finished"
You said with a yell!
With a yell, it is finished, for Death and Hell!

In three days and nights, the World made right
To be your Throne, given authority of your own
Baptism in water, Baptism in Blood
There is no greater honor, nor show of Love
What you gave to the World, were not worthy of
What you gave for the World, you gave out of pure Love
Thank you, Abba, for your Son, our Messiah
Who during judgment, will stand beside us
He'll make us righteous! by no deed of our own
So, we may all live
In his Abba's Home.

# Like Army Ants

**By Don Seick**

Time is a monster, or angle of life
Time isn't yours or mine, time belongs to no one
Time is un-forgiving, even cruel!
Time can be heartless, and leave you blue
Time is precious, for both, me and you
There is good time, and bad time, happy and sad time
Active time, and sleep time, laughing and crying time
Well spent time, and wasted time
The worst kind of time there is, is the time you lose
Living in sin, thinking you cool, being a fool
You can't retrieve one minute, of lost time
Like Army Ants, time marches on and on
You can do many things with time
But when time is lost, it's lost for good
And what you could, should or shouldn't have done or said
Right or wrong, only time will tell
You choose one, Heaven or hell
Be kind to time, because her hands, you can't bind or rewind
No one! Only Abba, controls the hands of time
His clock, is tic tock, ticking away, day by day
Bringing the world closer, in every way
To the righteousness of justice
In the judgment day!

# Little Girls, are the Future!

**By Don Seick**

Little girls cry
Little girls don't ask, or even wonder why, little girls die
Little girls die
By Filthy Satanic people! Ruining their lives
Little girls, are trying to stay alive, to survive!
They don't know, what they're doing or why they die
They don't understand, the greed
The perverted heartlessness, of a filthy, Satanic man
The people who buy and sell, rape and kill, little girls
Please dear Abba, the fire and brimstone of Hell itself is too good
For the Demons and Devils of this Satanic disease, may they
Never eat, sleep, or live in peace, for the little girls, who cry to die
From the horror they see, in these monster's eyes!
The terror, the terrified terror no one should feel
what these little girls go through, as these monsters rape and kill
They die by the hands of Satan's own, daughters and sons
Their just having Satan's own delusional, perverted Satanic fun!
They murder little girls and boys for sport!
OH, my God in Heaven, I can't wait till these Demonic people
End up in Heavens court!
Little girls, are the future, and the futures looking pretty bleak
When all about all the world, is about
How pretty little girls are!
As the moral character, towards the worlds little girls go
So too goes the world!

# Live for Today

**By Don Seick**

There is nothing to do
To change the things, life has handed you
The future, and today
Are going to throw things, in your way
Whether you're ready, like it or not
Living your life, you just can't stop!
You can't stop, the tears or hide from the fears
You can't stop the fact! This will probably go on for years
What you can and should do
Is to make up your mind, and decide for yourself
You're going to be fine, with a little help
What will you do? Cry your life away
Or live your life for today!
Abba, loves you, you know it's true
Don't you think, you could love you too?
Let the light of Messiah, dry the tears in your eyes
So, the light of Messiah, can shine through your life
Suffer, with him your daily pain
If you do, you can't lose, his love will remain
You can do it!
If with your heart, that's what you choose
Choose with your heart, and do it for you
And do it for him, who died for you too
I know it's not easy and may never be
So, if you need, you can always lean on me, You're in my prayers
Night and day, I know you'll choose Abba, and trust in his ways
And through his love, you'll see in yourself
A bright and shining, a new and better way!

# Made of Dust

**By Don Seick**

If a broken spirit dries the bones, then mine are made of dust
I guess that's why I don't walk, in the light of Messiah's love
But rather, in the dark of earthly lust
The word of Abba, and all his blessing's
It seems, were wasted, or lost on me, from the day I was born
I look at my life, and all I do is mourn
Feeling sorry for myself, ashamed! To the dust of my bones
My heart, completely torn
I fear the day, I'll look at you, and dread the things I've done
It's not that you can't or won't forgive me my sin's, It's me!
I don't, for some reason, I won't change! It seems I stay the same!
I look for a joy in my heart, to give my life a new start
That medicine from you, that will make my bones, stand alone
In the light, of your Heavenly eyes
Through the love, of shedding your blood
I'm sorry, to say the least, will you forgive me? To ask the most
My spirit, in the pit, I don't want to roast, but!
That will be nothing, compared to Eternity
Away from your Heavenly host! Thank you, Abba,
For the joy, you put in my heart, in my life, the blessing, of a new start
Only you, could give something so good, to someone like me
To be free from sin and pain
To be in Heaven, your Heavenly home
Eternal Eternity, never being alone.

# My Children?

**By Don Seick**

As I look around, throughout my world
I see life, death, and suffering! So much so, I know you love me
I love war! Murder, cold blooded murder, by the score!
Thank you, my children! I shouldn't ask for anything more?
Oh, but I will, and I do!
Because I can't stand you! I hate you! And you stupidly think I'm cool!
I wish you all, would rape, murder, and torture each other
Till the smell of death and rotting blood
Wipes out any and everything to do, with Heavens love
You will! Bow down and worship me
You will cry, beg, and plead on your knees, to me! For all your needs
And I? I will let you down
I will run, your rotting bones, into the blood soaked, rotting ground
Till there is nothing left
Not even your rotting bones to be found!
You steal, lie, and deny the truth for me, will you now
Help me turn this place, into a God forsaken de-humanized rat race?
Somewhere we can be without him
Who had the nerve to judge me!
I am Satan! Your Father, a friendless king!
And you all! Could be doing better for me
Now don't get me wrong, your almost there,
Like Sodom and Gamora, just a little bit more of
My filthy evil in your hearts, but we have to hurry! Times getting short!
Till God hold his Heavenly Court, you know he can't win, if I own
All his Women, Children, and Men, if you worship me, in time you'll
see
You! Stupid! dumb bastards, should have never listened to me!
Heavens only un-holy son
And inequity's Un-holy king!

# My Friend, He Told Me

**By Don Seick**

Dear Messiah, will you help me?
I know, I need help from you
So much changing in my life, I need, I want, I have to do
I'm lost in sin, blind to what's right
Seems my spirit moves through the night
Living my life to lose Women, drugs, and booze
Just some of the things I do to lose
Lying, stealing, deceiving who I can
All I see in myself, is an evilly satanic man
It's time to change, some call it repent
A friend, he told me, how you were sent
How to call on your name, for a chance to repent
If I call to you now, will you change me somehow?
Yahoshua Messiah, I call, I call to you now!
My friend he told me, how you gave your life
To be to all men, a bright and shining light
How they spilled your blood, because of your love
I wonder, I hope! Was it for me too?
Please tell me Messiah, what can and should I do?
If you don't save me, no one can
I'll be lost to the perversions of man
My friend he told me, you saved him for you
Please! Dear Messiah
Will you save me, for you too?

# Only You Can Reach Me

**By Don Seick**

Dear Abba, my Father
I'm beat up lonely and confused, like old dynamite
with a short rotten fuse
The world crowding in on me, my spirit, fighting my flesh
Running around and round, I trip and fall
Slamming! Me spiritually, to the ground
Lost in the dark, The Devil's home, beast of the earth!
I see, suffering and pain, I feel worse
Satan's working me hard, I'm being coerced!
Standing over me, like a triumphant beast!
My soul and spirit, he wants to eat
At times frightened, I know not what to do
To this beast, my soul, I don't want to lose
My guilt and shame, it's killer pain, in his house, I don't want to remain
Abba, my Father, I know you gave your Son, your only begotten one
He's the light of the world, to the world, he's life
Messiah, my master, how do I accept, the forgiveness in love
Provided for us, by the price of your Blood
Beating your body, ripping the flesh, exposing your bones
All your sufferings, through no fault of your own
In un-dying love, to accomplish the work, of the word above
All this, that man might be saved, from staying deaths slave
Knowing all this, the price you paid, why do I sin and not repent?
For in my life, by your Blood, you paid the rent
I do the thing's, I say, I don't like, I don't like the thing's, I say and do
I don't understand, why I'm such a fool, why do I do, what I do to you?
A hard, hearted man, is what I am
I'm turning to you now, Please, help me somehow, to say and do
The thing's that will bring me closer to you
I can't be away from you, not for a moment!

I must be a slave to you, or lost, in a moment
I guess, I think what I'm trying to say, is Messiah, my master
I need, I want, I must have you, every day, in your saving way
By your Abbas will, only you can teach me
Only you can reach me

# People of His Own

**By Don Seick**

Looking, always looking, looking to do what's right
Doing from the outside, what looks right
But from within the heart, where the truth presides
Is Wrong, Wrong, Wrong!
The battle is the same, all day long, the battle rages on
The shame remains, as the truth lives on
Did Abba put us here to do this and that?
And in our own righteous ways
To slap each other with pride on the back?
I don't know, but then again, I don't think so
I believe Abba put us here, for himself, so he could be with us!
People he could help, people he could love
people he just wants to take care of
I believe Abba just wants a family, people of his own
People who want to live with him, in his Heavenly home
But were not goanna get there, living wrong for right!
Lost to the love of Messiahs light
We're not gonna get there singing, a rationalized sad Satanic song
If that's the case, Stop! Step back! Take a look at yourself
What do you think, about what you see?
What do you feel, about how you feel?
By now, like me, you should feel ill
It's never too late to change, while you're in the here and now
It's never too late to pray, we've all got a part, in this world to play
And to look for those in the world, Abba, has put in our way
A loving, compassionate, understanding heart
And living in Abbas word, is a very good start
Salvation, in righteousness, has a price, it's not free
Messiahs Blood, paid the fee, to eternal life, For both, you and Me

# Plead of The Streets

**By Don Seick**

Save our streets and sleep in peace
Turning your head, turns them blood red
A Mothers dreams of peace and love
Her Children, are all she's thinking of
Guns and knives, gangs and chines
Blood and pain are all that remain, in the violence, of the street gangs
Drinking and drugs, fighting and dying, nationwide, nobody's trying
Look in our streets, at the kids you can meet
Their hearts so hungry, the evil they see, is the evil they be
Eyes so black, they make the night seem bright
All you people filled with fright!
The time is at hand, we must make a stand
Right or wrong, we got to choose, this can't go on or we all lose
Our Government! Is looking for war!
We must say No! our war is at home
In the streets, of the freest land, Men and Women have ever known
Plead of the streets, our kids are dead meat
Guns and knives, Gangs and chines
Blood and pain are all that remain
It's murder from the start, if we don't find some heart
The Olé Red White and Blue, our Country, is counting on Me and
You!
To do what needs to be done
For our Nations Daughters and Sons

# Shalom

**By Don Seick**

You have reached the voice mail of
Yahova
The almighty Abba of creation
I'm not in at this time, nor have I been
Since the common era began
I am however, still sustaining all life
I may be out among the Heavenly lights
Or anywhere in my creation, as a matter of fact
I will be back at my prescribed time
If, you have any questions, needs, or prayers
Or if you just want to talk
Please contact my Son, Yahoshua
He will, and is very able to take care of all your needs
Till my return
Your Abba, Shalom

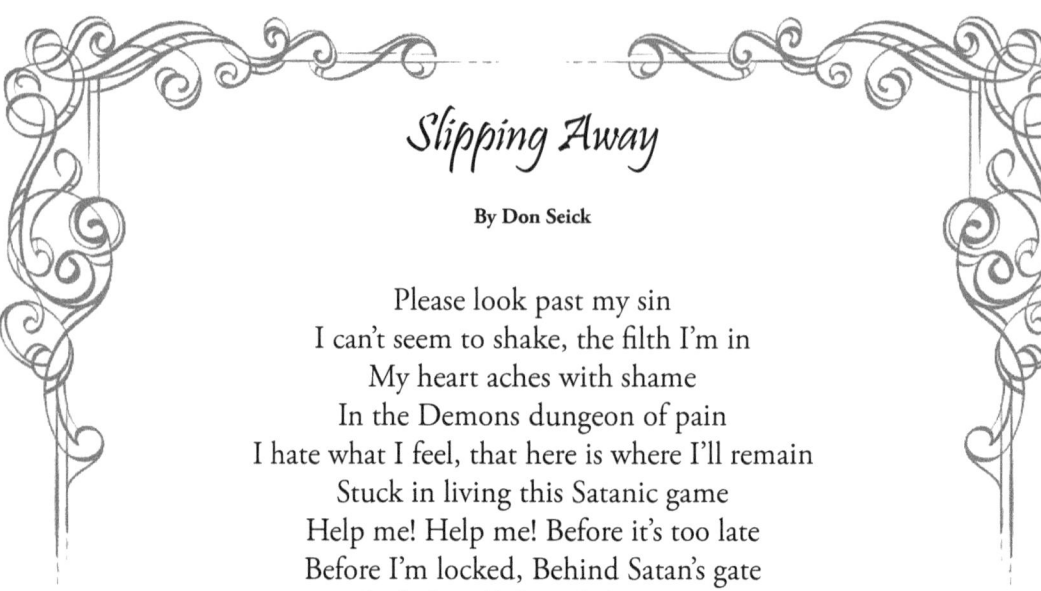

# Slipping Away

**By Don Seick**

Please look past my sin
I can't seem to shake, the filth I'm in
My heart aches with shame
In the Demons dungeon of pain
I hate what I feel, that here is where I'll remain
Stuck in living this Satanic game
Help me! Help me! Before it's too late
Before I'm locked, Behind Satan's gate
The light of life, is fading away
As I watch Messiah, slipping away.

# So Little and Defenseless

**By Don Seick**

The innocent unborn are people too
I don't understand a Woman's, so called right to choose
They never had that right, and never will
It's not a woman's right to choose who to Kill!
Abba our EL, puts life into the womb
Don't turn that life into a deadly wound!
Killing your babies and stripping them clean
Then burning their bodies, is far beyond mean, It's;
Evilly Cruel, and Satanically Nasty!
Abba's, keeping count, he knows the score
He knows where he sends them and a whole lot more
He knows the thoughts, of your heart and soul
Someday, you won't be so selfishly bold
As you'll stand before Abba, our God! And you'll stand alone
And at his feet, your Babies will adore him
They'll look at you, remembering no pain
With Abba, their Father they know, they'll remain
You'll look at your Baby, and into Abba's eyes
You'll have to explain in truth and no lies
Why you, Murdered his Baby
So little and defenseless
May leave you
A little Defenseless!

# Sounds of Time

**By Don Seick**

Open your eyes and look around
Do you hear the sounds of time going by?
Do you even care or wonder why?
Could Sodom and Gamora, have been worse than today?
I wonder in what and in how many ways
The killings, not just killings, but cold-blooded murder
By cold-blooded, black hearted people, who will look you in the eye
As they watch your life run dry and die
People, who for their own Mother, wouldn't cry
The rapes, the beatings, so much violence all around
So many people being walked on, like dirt on the ground!
We're living on the edge of time, tomorrow is promised to no one
Sharp, is the edge of time, it will cut you off with no warning
Yesterday, what you should have did or said
Today, you won't be able to do or say
Time is wasting away! The sharp edge of time
Wasting away day after day, time is promised to no one
Don't you see?
The Sun, the Moon, the Heavens, and Stars
The whole Earth, is filled with Satanic scars
Abba's word is coming like a two-edged sword!
The Sword of Justice, the Sword of Righteousness,
They are, The Swords of Vengeance, the only Sword
That can cut, through the edge of time!

# Spiritual Breeze and Me

**By Don Seick**

Thank you, Abba, for the spirit that lifted our hearts
Out of the dark
The heavens and earth, have witnessed our shame
Thank you, Messiah for taking our blame
Without you, we are nothing but the dust of the Earth
You said, the dust is the Serpents food
Food of the Serpent is what we'd be
If you hadn't saved the Breeze and me
Thank you, Abba, for the joy in our lives
The joy in our hearts
At the tear of the curtain, you gave us a new start
Like the Sun, the Moon, and the Stars so high
In our spiritual lives so are the Breeze and I
The way we'd like to spend our days
Is with the Angles singing you praise
You're the light in the World, that brightens our hearts
Your word is the light, for the World from the start
Your spirit has given the World to be, and out of the Sea
You picked, the Breeze and me
Were so happy there's no words to say
How our hearts long for that Blessed day
When you from Heave will be on your way
To do in this World by the price you paid
Thank you, Yahoshua, our EL, for all we see
For all your Blessings on the Breeze and me!

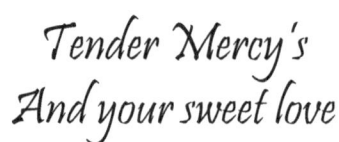

# Tender Mercy's
# And your sweet love

**By Don Seick**

I'm no longer tedder tottering, on the edge of spiritual death
I'm hanging over the wall of the pit
And I'm hanging by a thread
As the fire grows higher and higher, it becomes hotter and hotter
To save the likes of me? Why would you bother!
So many others out there, who deserve to call you Father
I know in my life; I've had plenty of times
To say and do what's right
But I've let you down time after time
No other to fault, the blame is mine
I truly fear for my life, not the one in flesh!
But the one that counts, the one of your Son's death
My Spiritualness!
It's on the line, a matter of time
I wonder again and again about time
Is there time, enough time
For your sanctification on me to shine
To save me from myself
I'm tired of lying, tired of trying
To put the blame on someone else
If I'm judged by the righteousness of justice
From the fires flame, I'll receive eternal pain
And only me, myself to blame
Judgment by mercy is my hope from you
To wash away my wrongful ways
To help me now, to spare me somehow
In your kind and loving way
Sorry to bother you, but I feel I have no choice
Or I'll be lost to Ha-Satan, and he will be my voice!
You said "Before they call, I will answer
While they are still speaking, I will hear"

You said "The dust, will be the serpent's food"
Abba, if I fall into the pit, I'll be the serpent's food!
Upon your Mountain, I plead, my need from you
But I need your hand up too
Through Messiah, your Sons Blood
Through Messiah, you show your love
In the words of King David;
"Please save me by your tender mercy, and your sweet love"
In the Justice, of the Judgment Day

# The Beauty, Of Your Story

**By Don Seick**

Abba, my Father, I'm lost without you
No matter what happens day to day
The things that go on, and the things people say
They can't get me down, if I remember to pray
I wake up in the morning, to your beautiful Sunrise
As you show me your story, tears fill my eyes
I can feel your Glory all around
Though sometimes I can't help it, life gets me down
Before I know it, I'm wearing a frown
Feeling sad and blue, that's when you do it, bring me back to you!
I take a deep breath, and my nerves calm down
I can see your blessings, are all around
Here comes that Sunrise, east of town
Thank you, Abba, for never letting me down
These are all the blessings; I wish all people could see
The blessings I found, when you called me
By opening my eyes, I can't deny, your power and Glory
The Beauty of Your Story
Your loving compassion and long suffering
Through Messiah Yahoshua, our sins white as snow
Again, he'll come, and there's only one way to know!
Out of the darkness, on a cloud he'll descend
Like lightening that covers the sky
Messiah, will be coming for you and I
With the sound of a trumpet, by mouth, his Angle Gabriel will shout!
Throughout all the Earth, there won't be a doubt
Messiah Yahoshua, Son of El, has been seen
He brings mercy for all, who answered the call
Through the power of the spirit from on high
Salvation! He brings as the Angles will sing
A Heavenly song, as to with El for Eternity, we will all belong
Abba, my Father, what a wonderful plan
What a Beautiful Story, you enacted through Man!

# The Devil's Home

**By Don Seick**

I'm going to Hell, to Gehenna!
Not going to the peace of Heaven
But, to the tormenting torment of Gehenna
I'll be the worm that doesn't die
The smoke, that rises forever in the sky
The unquenchable fire, burning in my heart
The result of my life, a failure from the start
So much potential, like unfinished art
I'm going to Hell, Gehenna, home of the dark
The birthplace of loneliness, anger, and despair
Final resting place of death, pain, and those who don't care
Only the burning;
The Oh so slow burning of my soul, within my smoking bones
I'm going to Hell, Gehenna, the Devils home!
Where Abba and the Angles will leave me alone, all alone
Forever more alone, in the Devils home
Me, in forever's torment, me and my smoking bones
In Un-equity's Un- holy home

# The Human Game

**By Don Seick**

Were black and white, red, yellow, and brown
Male and Female, were all being put down
The money, the bling all the riches I've seen
Being put down, by those who look so good and smell so clean
Behind the smile, A heart so cold, there evil so bold
It doesn't matter who or how old they are anymore
Green is the only matter of color, that matters anymore
All of you fools who think, your too cool for rules
At what cost, the price of life? Living, dying, laughing, or crying
It makes no difference, when nobody's trying!
The mood of the country, in the world it's the same
In drug's, booze and killing, there is no shame!
Godless political corruption is mostly to blame
How long will this violence, continue to go on?
Is there anyone out there who really does care, anyone at all!
With each other, the truth you're willing to share?
Go on Y'all, keep doing your thing
Till the God of Heaven hears the Earth scream!
Gods goanna be ticked, when he says "That's it" payday is someday
For all our 'butts' will run out of luck
And the price will be too high to pay!
It's time to get right, not only for yourself
But for those along the way
It's up to you, win or lose, it really does matter in the way you choose
Were all people in flesh and blood, were all equal in Abbas love
Were all equal through a human hug
Without these two things, death and pain is all that remains
In the heartless world of the human game!

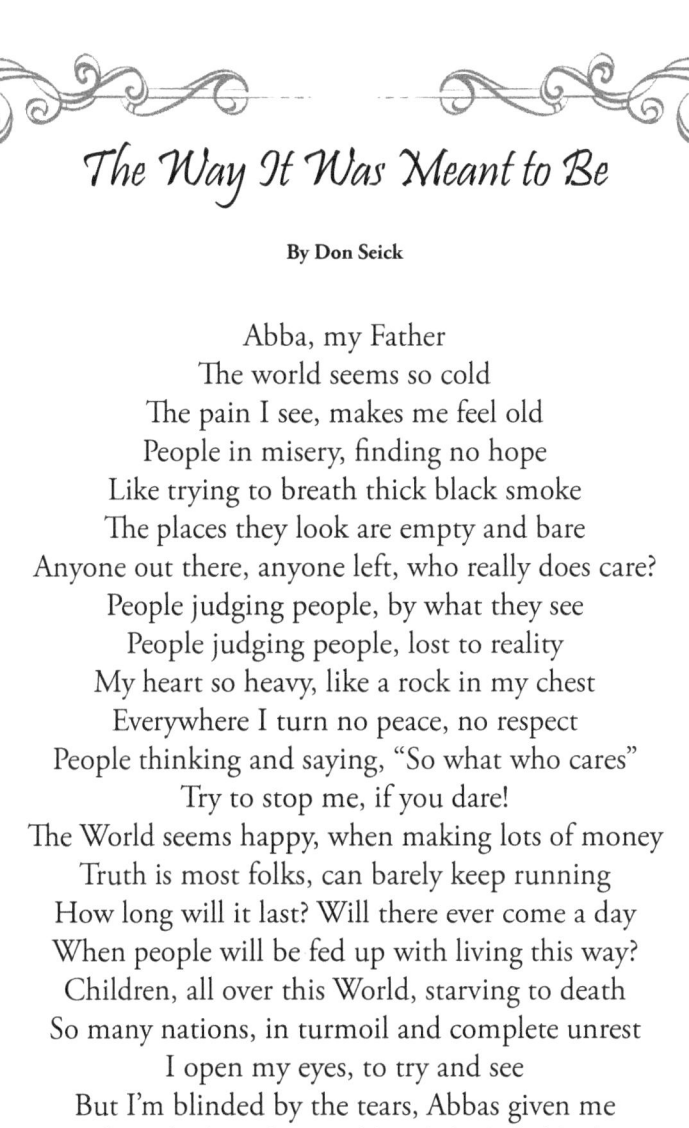

# The Way It Was Meant to Be

**By Don Seick**

Abba, my Father
The world seems so cold
The pain I see, makes me feel old
People in misery, finding no hope
Like trying to breath thick black smoke
The places they look are empty and bare
Anyone out there, anyone left, who really does care?
People judging people, by what they see
People judging people, lost to reality
My heart so heavy, like a rock in my chest
Everywhere I turn no peace, no respect
People thinking and saying, "So what who cares"
Try to stop me, if you dare!
The World seems happy, when making lots of money
Truth is most folks, can barely keep running
How long will it last? Will there ever come a day
When people will be fed up with living this way?
Children, all over this World, starving to death
So many nations, in turmoil and complete unrest
I open my eyes, to try and see
But I'm blinded by the tears, Abbas given me
If you look at this world and don't feel bad
Then Brothers and Sisters, for you too, I feel sad
Abba, my Father, I must say
I pray for the World, I pray for the day
When I'll look toward Heaven, and I'll hear you say
"It's over, No more tears! There's a new and better way
Come here to me!
And I'll show you the World, the way it was meant to be"

# This Confusing Day

**By Don Seick**

As I lay here in bed, thinking
Of all the things I've done and said
About all the people, who have put a bullet, in their heads
By pulling the trigger of a gun
They must have been sad and Oh, so lonely
They must have been thinking of themselves only
Cold but true, not thinking of you
And all in their lives, you're waiting to do
I've been there, I know that despair, the gun in my hand
Abba, you've been good to me, the sinner I am, kind in every way
Shame, for the way I've lived my life, at times, I feel, I must pay
Would anyone notice?  would anyone care?
Would anyone, with my messed-up self, really want to share?
BANG! It's over, no more pain, BANG! It's over, no more shame
Not till the day, not till the last trumpet, the angles will play
Announcing you, our Messiah, is on his way
Then I'd get up to the pain of shame, Quitting, would be waiting for
me
I'd look at you then hang my head, having nothing to say
Knowing, I through, life's chances away
So, I'll just live for today, and hope for tomorrow
And try to stop walling, in my sorrow
Remembering, the Sun's gonna rise, and maybe me too!
But, if I pull that trigger, I know I lose
My Dear Messiah, through your love, by your Blood
I'm reaching for you and mercy too
Please show me the way, save me from myself
In this confound! and confusing day

# Till Your Blessings Are Mine

**By Don Seick**

Abba, my Father, it's happening like the good book said
The wolves have come in, Satan's temptations burning my head
I'm fighting, battling, I'm torn up inside!
There's nothing to decide
This evil in me, I don't want to survive
I meant what I said
your commandments turning my head, to do what's right
I beg, I plead my needs, on my knees I cry!
How much longer will it be?
Will you ever, or are you now answering me?
I'm waiting in your time, wanting it now
Knowing your time, is best somehow
It was better said by one greater than I
Who's sandals I'm not fit to untie
"Not by my will Abba" said your Son
But "Let your will be done"
I'll keep fighting, battling, trying to stand the test of time
I'll keep praying and trying to find
All your Blessings, till all your Blessings are mine

# Who's Your Abba?

**By Don Seick**

Gehenna is a place stoked with desire
A burning fire, of human desire
To be somewhere else, anywhere else
Then in this pit, with the King! Of all Gehenna's liars
For every un-saved soul, this will be home
You won't have to worry, you won't be alone
You'll be with every Rapist and low life Killer of Women and Children
All the dregs of society too! And there's nothing you can do
But to think and reflect, of the lives you wrecked!
Seeing Abba, the Angles in Heaven, or your family too?
Forget it!
For throughout all Eternity, this will never happen for you!
You'll be alone, with your thoughts and shame
And no one will care, you've only yourself to blame
Your misery, will be yours alone to bare!
if after a few Billion years or so, the loneliness gets you down
Turn around, you won't be alone after all!
Your friends will be there too, to welcome you home
The false Prophet, Anti-messiah, and Oh yeah! Don't forget!
Your Father Satan the Devil! Will be there too
Your Father the Devil, will be there to forever torment you
To the dust, of all your burning desires
In Gehenna, the Un-quenchable fire

# Who Paid the Rent!

**By Don Seick**

My gosh, this World is awful nasty, mean and cruel
It seems all wrong, in all that I see we do
People in pain searching for gain
At the end of day, broken hearts, are all that remain
Evil, is the game the World wants to play
Evil, is the way the World wants to stay
I get afraid when I look around, because I know
Abbas anger, is goanna bring it all down, Abbas burning anger
Again, will burn so hot, it'll make the Sun seem cold!
Most of us folks, won't live to grow old
According to Revelation, it's all said and done
Except, for the suffering, to be experienced by some
If Abba treated us, like we treat our children
Our souls are on the bubble! Were in trouble!
We spoil our kids, buy what they want
We make excesses for their wrongs, all day long
No fear, no disciplines tears
Abba said "You hate your Kids, if you spare the rod"
If you don't teach them right from wrong
The streets will! so many people, the streets  Kill!
Don't get me wrong, Abba loves us all
And were all gonna see just how much
When Abba brings his wrath down, on all of us!
Like Sodom and Gamora, fire and brimstone!
No water, no food, what Abbas gonna do
Will make the World choke!
Again! Like trying to breath, thick black smoke
If you'll look, at the worldly signs, you'll know there's not much time
Fall to your knees, as you pray and plead, for the need to repent!
And while you're at it, thank Abba for his Son, the Messiah he sent
Who, by his Blood, has paid the rent!

Wisdom is to fear El

To fear El, is to love El

To love El is to love his commandments

To obey Els commandments

Is to show understanding

To show understanding, is to please El

To please El, is wisdom

Solman said,

The one who sleeps with evil

Shall wake with evil in his heart!


Shalom

That if you confess with your mouth,

your belief in the Master

'Ya ho shua' is the Son of God

and believe in your heart that

Elohime has raised Him from the dead,

YOU SHALL BE SAVED!

Now go get Baptized in the

Name of the Father:"Ya ho va"

The Son: "Ya ho shua"

And the Spirit: "Ruach Hakha Dosh!"

You are now Baptized into the,

Death and Resurrection of the Messiah!

Romans 10:9